Scott, Foresman Social Studies

The photograph on the cover is of
a mural painted by school children
on a railroad underpass in Chicago.

Scott, Foresman
SOCIAL STUDIES

Dr. Joan Schreiber
Professor of History
(Social Studies Methods)
Ball State University
Muncie, Indiana

Scott, Foresman and Company
Editorial Offices: Glenview, Illinois

Regional Sales Offices: Palo Alto, California •
Tucker, Georgia • Glenview, Illinois •
Oakland, New Jersey • Dallas, Texas

Program Development

Dr. Joan Schreiber
Professor of History
(Social Studies Methods)
Ball State University
Muncie, Indiana

William Stepien
Head, Social Studies Department
School District No. 300
Dundee, Illinois

Dr. Geneva Gay
Associate Professor of Education
Purdue University
West Lafayette, Indiana

Dr. Alan J. Hoffman
Associate Professor of Education
Georgia State University
Atlanta, Georgia

Authors

Dr. Roger M. Berg
Associate Professor
Elementary Education
The University of Nebraska
at Omaha
Omaha, Nebraska

Randee Blair
Teacher—Orrington School
Evanston, Illinois

Dan D'Amelio
Instructional Materials Specialist
Special Education Resource Center
Hartford, Connecticut

Joyce H. Frank
Teacher—Haslett Public Schools
Haslett, Michigan

Dr. Richard K. Jantz
Associate Professor
Department of Early Childhood
Elementary Education
University of Maryland
College Park, Maryland

Judith Medoff
Teacher—Central School
Evanston, Illinois

Dr. Barbara M. Parramore
Associate Professor and Head
Department of Curriculum
and Instruction
School of Education
North Carolina State University
at Raleigh
Raleigh, North Carolina

Dr. Joan Schreiber
Professor of History
(Social Studies Methods)
Ball State University
Muncie, Indiana

Dr. Richard E. Servey
Professor of Elementary Education
San Diego State University
San Diego, California

Priscilla Smith
Teacher—Orrington School
Evanston, Illinois

William Stepien
Head, Social Studies Department
School District No. 300
Dundee, Illinois

Teacher Consultants

Linda Bohan
Teacher—Jordan Acres School
Brunswick, Maine

Barbara Briggs
Teacher—Washington School
Plainfield, New Jersey

Melba F. Coleman
Project Director
Wonders of Work Project
Fifty-Second Street Elementary
School
Los Angeles, California

Althea Cooper
Teacher—Esmond School
Chicago, Illinois

Sue Crow
Teacher—Floydada Public Schools
Floydada, Texas

Marie de Porres, I.H.M.
Teacher—St. Madeline Convent
Ridley Park, Pennsylvania

Frank Espinoza
Teacher—Sierra Vista Elementary
School
Clovis, California

Richard Follett
Environmental Consultant
Public Schools
Santa Rosa, California

Charlie Mae Hutchings
Social Studies Specialist
Chattanooga Public Schools
Chattanooga, Tennessee

Helen Jenkins
Consultant
Nu-Ma-Ku Alternative School
Freeport, New York

Sally Klepack
Teacher—Edgar L. Miller School
Merrillville, Indiana

Alan McAtee
Teacher—Rattlesnake School
Missoula, Montana

Dr. Dorothy J. Mugge
Professor of Early Childhood
Education
Shippensburg State College
Shippensburg, Pennsylvania

Dr. Arthur S. Nichols
Associate Professor of Elementary
Education
California State University
Northridge, California

Barbara Okimoto
Teacher—Burnett Jr. High School
San Jose, California

David Silva
Teacher—Montebello School
Phoenix, Arizona

Marie S. Strickland
Teacher—Donald J. Richey School
Wilmington, Delaware

Serena Westbrook
Teacher—William Paca Elementary
School
Landover, Maryland

Dr. Nancy Wyner
Assistant Professor for Teacher
Education/Social Science
Wheelock College
Boston, Massachusetts

ISBN: 0 673 11611 5

Copyright © 1979,
Scott, Foresman and Company, Glenview, Illinois.
All Rights Reserved.
Printed in the United States of America.

The Acknowledgment Section on page 200 is an extension of the copyright page.

2345678910-RRW-888786858483828180799

Contents

UNIT

1

Doing and Deciding   2

Lesson 1   The Person You Are   4
Lesson 2   All on Your Own   8
Lesson 3   Inside of You   16
When You Read: Word Meanings   20
Unit Test   22

UNIT

2

Things, Places, and People   24

Lesson 1   At the Zoo   26
Environment: Protecting Our Wildlife   30
Lesson 2   The Right Place, The Right Time   32
When You Read: Cardinal Directions   38
Lesson 3   A Funny Feeling   44
Lesson 4   Little Arabella Miller   50
Unit Test   52

UNIT

3

Needs and Wants 54

Lesson 1	Mr. Lucky Straw	56
When You Read: Finding the Main Idea		62
Lesson 2	Getting Needs and Wants	64
Consumer Concerns: Paying for Wants and Needs		68
Lesson 3	Becky's Band	70
Unit Test		76

UNIT

4

Belonging to Groups 78

Lesson 1	Racing Turtles	80
Lesson 2	Another Leader	84
Lesson 3	Snowed In	86
When You Read: Reading Articles		92
Lesson 4	Eduardo's Community	94
Unit Test		102

UNIT

5

Alike and Different   104

Lesson 1   Games Around the World   106
Lesson 2   Family Groups   110
Lesson 3   Something New   114
When You Read: Getting the Big Idea   118
Lesson 4   The Long Recess   120
Unit Test   122

UNIT

6

Being Yourself in Groups   124

Lesson 1   Ricardo   126
Lesson 2   A Community Problem   132
Careers: Community Workers   134
Lesson 3   You Have Rights   136
When You Read: What's Important?   147
Unit Test   148

UNIT

7

Making Changes   150

Lesson 1   The Way Things Used to Be:
           A Play   152
Lesson 2   Mike's Report   158
When You Read: Reading Charts   164
Lesson 3   The Wild Horses   166
Law: How Is a Law Made in Washington?   172
Unit Test   176

Handbook of
Skills and Information   178

Getting New Information   179
Practicing Map and Globe Skills   182
Words to Know   194
Index   198

Scott, Foresman Social Studies

Unit 1 Doing and Deciding

3

Lesson 1 The Person You Are

4

You can do many things.
·The things you do help people know you.

You can play.
You can joke and laugh.
You can run and chase.

You can work.

Joe and Rachel are working. They are fixing their wagon.

You can make things.

Tim and Lee are making a bowl.
You play, work, and make things.
The things you do show what kind
of person you are.

7

Lesson 2   All on Your Own

You can decide some things.

Maria decided to paint a picture. The picture shows how Maria feels.

"Look at the picture I painted. I love horses. I like to ride. I'm proud of my painting."

Al decided to clean up after painting. First he had fun and played. Now he is working.

Tony decided to play alone for a while.

What would you decide to do?

Carla's Pool

Carla's house is near a pool. Her family often goes there to swim. Today Carla's parents cannot go swimming. They have other things to do.

Carla wants to swim in the pool. Her parents want her to be safe. Mother says, "You may not swim there alone, Carla."

13

But the sun is hot. Carla is alone. "No one will know," she thinks. "What should I do?" Carla wonders.

What do you think Carla should do?

14

15

Lesson 3   Inside of You

Suppose you felt lonely. You might say:

When I feel lonely
　　Then I sit
All by myself
　　And think a bit,
And ask myself
　　Why is it true
That certain times
　　I feel so blue?
　　　　William Wise

16

Suppose you felt happy. You might want to
jump and yell.

Sometimes you feel proud. Tracy feels
proud. Later she will tell her mother, "I got
a hit! I helped our team win the game!"

You can show how you feel.

When You Read

You can find new ideas in words. But be careful. Words can have more than one meaning.

Remember the poem on page 16. The last line was "I feel so blue." The word "blue" may be a color. But it may also tell about a feeling. When people feel blue, they feel unhappy.

Here are other words with more than one meaning.
Tell how the underlined word in sentence **a** is
different from the underlined word in sentence **b**.

1. **a.** The ocean <u>wave</u> came to the shore.
   b. The children gave their grandmother
   a <u>wave</u> goodbye.

2. **a.** The boy and girl followed <u>directions</u> to
   make the cake.
   b. First the man went north; then he
   changed <u>direction</u>.

3. **a.** The man wore a <u>tie</u>.
   b. The race ended in a <u>tie</u>.

What Do You Know?

Find the pictures that go with the words.

happy

lonely

proud

Ideas to Know

What are the people in these pictures doing?

Using What You Know

Look at the picture. Tell who has decided to act safely and who has not. Tell why you answer as you do. Why might people sometimes not act safely?

Unit 2 Things, Places, and People

Lesson 1   At the Zoo

What a day to be at the zoo!
Pete, Beth, and Jan are early.
The gate is closed. A sign tells
when the zoo will open.

"Only a few minutes more,"
says Beth.

26

ZOO CLOSED

OPEN 9:00 A.M. TO 5:00 P.M.

Sixty seconds
Pass in a minute.
Sixty minutes
Pass in an hour.
Twenty-four hours
Pass in a day—
And that's how TIME
Keeps passing away!

Ilo Orleans

27

At the petting zoo, the children get to hold
some of the animals. They like the warm,
soft rabbits best.

28

BE GENTLE

THE ANIMALS
DO NOT LIKE
TO BE SQUEEZED!

Sometimes things around
you show you what to do.
Gates, signs, and clocks
showed the children what,
when, and how to do
things.

Protecting Our Wildlife

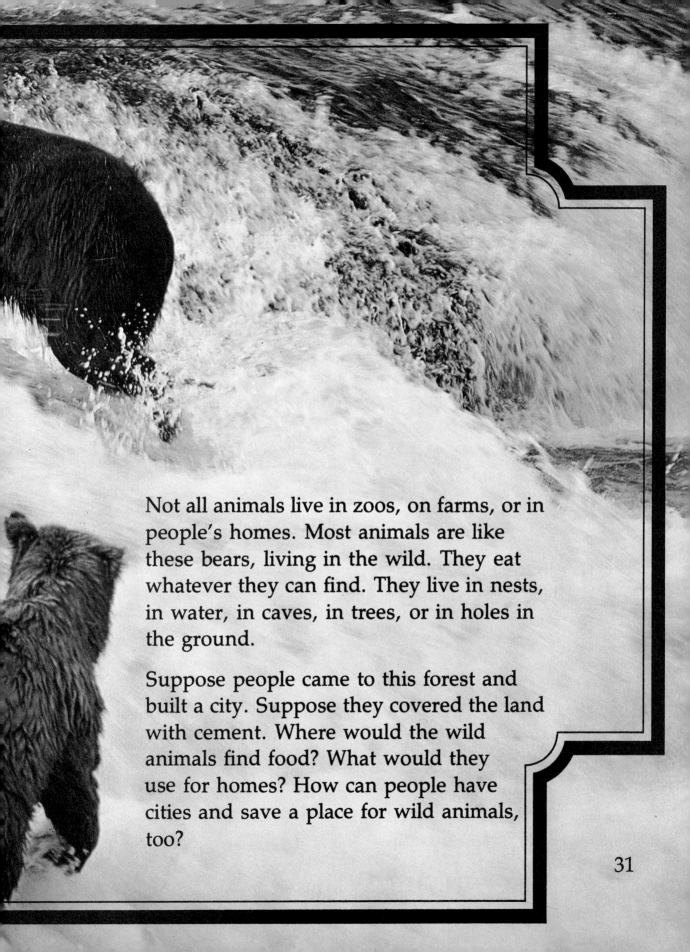

Not all animals live in zoos, on farms, or in people's homes. Most animals are like these bears, living in the wild. They eat whatever they can find. They live in nests, in water, in caves, in trees, or in holes in the ground.

Suppose people came to this forest and built a city. Suppose they covered the land with cement. Where would the wild animals find food? What would they use for homes? How can people have cities and save a place for wild animals, too?

Lesson 2 The Right Place, The Right Time

"Ssh-ssh! I came to read a book. Don't
make a sound. Don't rush and run
around."

"Get a bat! Let's play some ball! Let's jump and run and yell!"

Some places are right for reading. Others are good for playing ball. Where you are makes a difference in what you do.

Some places have a certain kind of weather.

Weather makes a difference in what you do.

Some places have a
certain kind of land.

Land makes a difference
in what you do.

When You Read

You can tell where you are from a map. And maps can help you get where you want to go. Bear found that out.

This note was nailed to Bear's door one morning.

This note told Bear how to use the map.

Directions

1. Go <u>east</u> on Forest Lane, past the school, to Rabbit Drive.

2. Go <u>south</u> on Rabbit Drive to the food store. Then turn <u>west</u> on Raccoon Way.

3. Pass the fire house and go <u>south</u> on Field Mouse Street to the X.

40

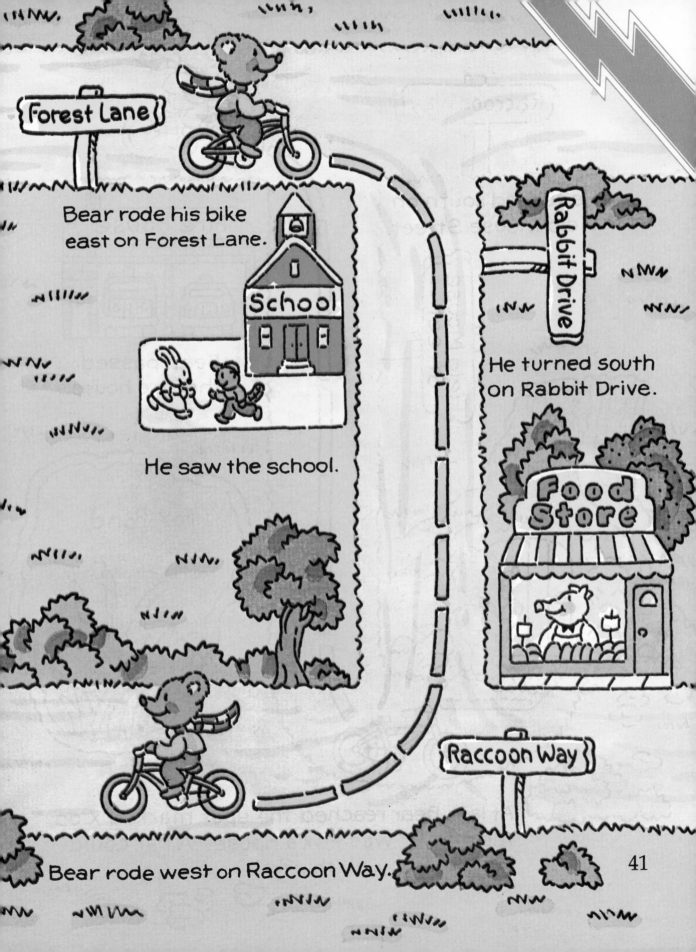

Bear rode his bike
east on Forest Lane.

He saw the school.

He turned south
on Rabbit Drive.

Bear rode west on Raccoon Way.

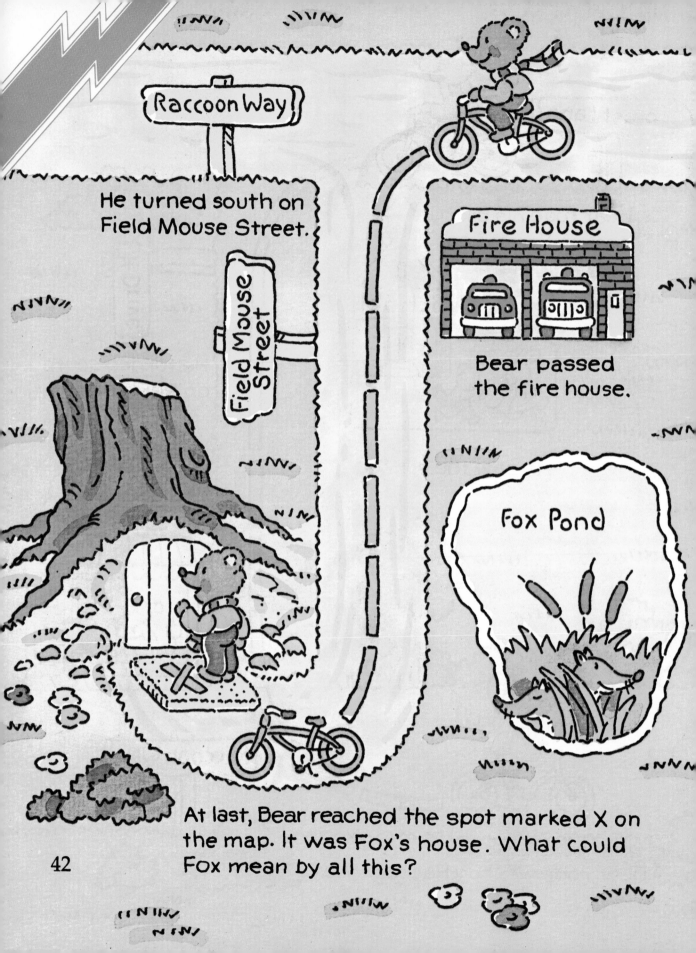

Raccoon Way

He turned south on
Field Mouse Street.

Field Mouse Street

Fire House

Bear passed
the fire house.

Fox Pond

At last, Bear reached the spot marked X on
the map. It was Fox's house. What could
Fox mean by all this?

"Surprise, Bear! Happy Birthday! We're glad you found the way."

43

Lesson 3
A Funny Feeling

"Dad, I scored two runs today!" Janie said.
"I even caught a fly ball."

Her father only said, "Oh." He didn't seem
to be listening.

Janie was puzzled. She thought, "Usually
he wants to know about my baseball
games."

44

"OK, let's eat now," Father said.

"Aren't we going to wait for Mom?" Janie asked.

"No, let's just start. I don't know when she'll be home," said her father.

Janie wondered where her mother was. She began to get a funny feeling. Suddenly she didn't feel like eating anymore.

45

"Mom, where were you?" Janie cried.

"Oh, Janie, your father and I argued over something silly. I needed to get away. I went for a long walk."

"Yes, it was a silly thing to argue about. Let's forget it happened," Father said.

Then Janie's father said, "People in a family can get angry sometimes, Janie, but they still love one another."

Suddenly Janie felt very hungry. "Pass the potatoes, please. I'm starving."

47

The people in your family influence you.
Friends influence you, too.

"Tommy, thanks for watching my store
while I was gone. It's good to have a friend
I can depend on."

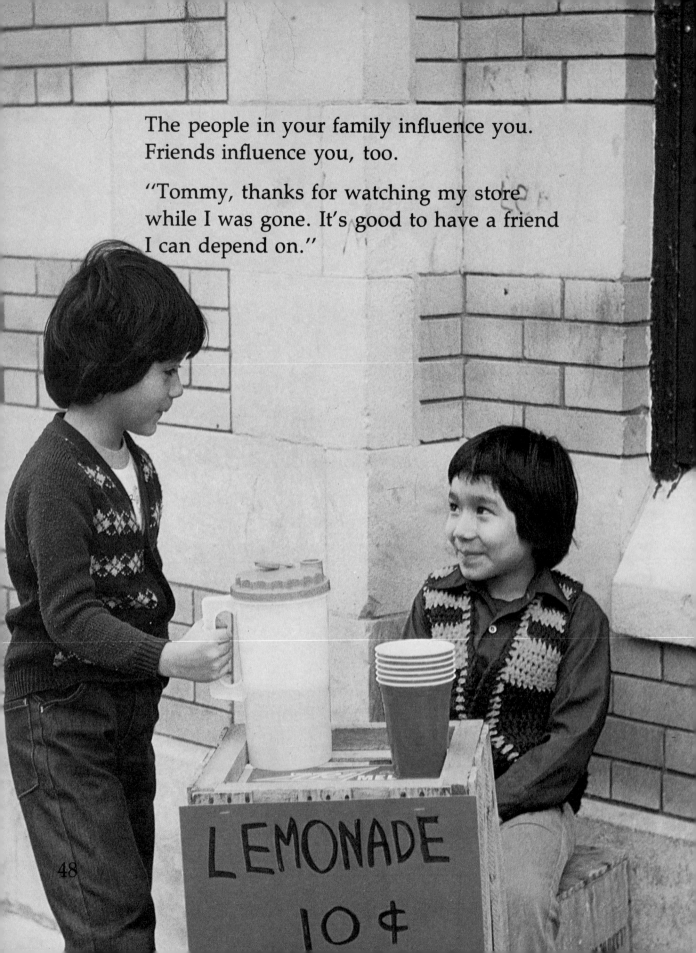

48

LEMONADE
10¢

What neighbors do can affect you.
"I'm sorry, Mr. Green. I'll fix your flowers
as good as new."

49

Lesson 4 Little Arabella Miller

Little Arabella Miller
   Found a woolly caterpillar.
First it crawled upon her mother
   Then upon her baby brother;
All said, "Arabella Miller,
   Take away that caterpillar."

50

25 / LITTLE ARABELLA MILLER

Rather slow

Words: Anon. Music: Adapted

Lit - tle Ar - a - bel - la Mill - er found a wool - ly cat - ter - pil - lar.

First it crawled up - on her moth - er, then up - on her ba - by broth - er;

All said, "Ar - a - bel - la Mill - er, take a - way that cat - er - pil - lar."

Things and people can affect you. But what you do can affect others. Arabella Miller found that out!

What Do You Know?

Words to Know

Find the pictures that go with the words.

family

friends

neighbor

map

directions

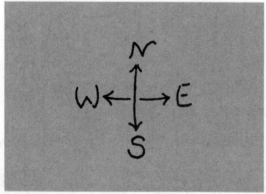

Ideas to Know

What do you think is the most important sentence on page 47? Say the idea that is in that sentence, this time in your own words.

Using What You Know

Here are some pictures of different kinds of weather. Say a sentence about how each kind of weather might affect you. What can you do to be comfortable in such weather?

53

Unit **3** Needs and Wants

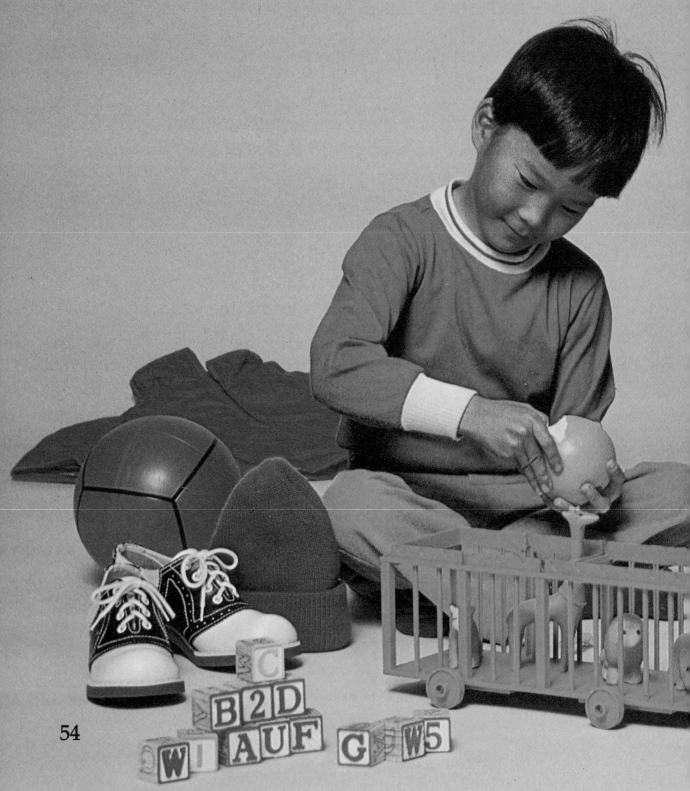

Lesson 1   Mr. Lucky Straw

The story "Mr. Lucky Straw" was first told long ago in Japan. Then people lived differently than they do today. Yet the people then had needs and wants just as they do now. Read "Mr. Lucky Straw."

Once upon a time, in a village in Japan, there lived a boy named Shobei. One day, as Shobei walked home from the fields, he tripped and fell. A long piece of straw stuck on his hand.

Farther down the road, a dragonfly
bothered Shobei. He caught the dragonfly
and tied it to the straw.

Then a little boy saw Shobei's dragonfly on
the piece of straw. The boy said, "Mother, I
want the dragonfly."

So, the woman traded three oranges for
Shobei's dragonfly.

57

A little later, Shobei met a traveler. The traveler was thirsty. But there was no water nearby. The traveler said, "I need your juicy oranges. I will give you three pieces of cloth for them."

So, Shobei traded the oranges for the cloth.

58

After that, Shobei met a rich princess. The princess wanted the pieces of cloth. She said, "Give me the beautiful cloth. In return, I will give you a bag of money."

So, Shobei traded the cloth for the money.

Shobei took the money to his village. He
divided it among his people. The people
used the money to buy the things they
needed and wanted.

They never forgot that Shobei shared his
money. The people honored Shobei and
always called him Mr. Lucky Straw.

Everyone has needs and wants. In the story, the child wanted a toy. The traveler needed a drink. The princess wanted the cloth. The people in Shobei's town needed lots of things.

Needs are things you can't live without. Food, clothes, and a home are needs. So are love and safety. Wants are things that may be nice to have. A toy, a candy bar, or a movie show are wants.

When You Read

You can learn a lot from the story, "Mr. Lucky Straw." You can learn to:
1. read to answer questions.
2. read to find the main idea.

1. Answer these questions about "Mr. Lucky Straw."
   a. What did the woman give Shobei in return for the dragonfly?
   b. What did the traveler give to Shobei?
   c. What did Shobei do with his money?

2. Pick the sentence that says the main idea of the story, "Mr. Lucky Straw."
   a. Little boys like dragonflies tied to pieces of straw.
   b. Travelers are thirsty people.
   c. People have many needs and wants.

Lesson 2   Getting Needs and Wants

The people in the story, "Mr. Lucky Straw,"
got the things they needed and wanted.
They traded something for them. Or they
bought them with money. Or someone
gave them what they needed and wanted.

You, too, may get some of the things you
need and want in these ways.

But other needs and wants you can't buy.
Think of your loved ones or of a friend you
can depend on or of playing at the beach.
These are things you can't buy.

PAYING FOR NEEDS AND WANTS

How do we get some of the needs and wants we can buy?

Parents get money from work.

They spend some of
the money on

food,

clothes,

housing.

They may take the
family on vacation.

They may buy you a toy.

They may save some
of the money for
an emergency.

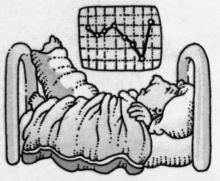

69

Lesson 3
Becky's Band

Becky wanted to
play a tambourine.
She didn't have
one. So, this is
what she did.

Step 1
Becky gathered
together:

a used, thin metal pie pan

a tool for punching
holes in the pan

string

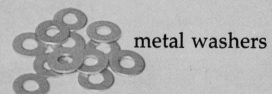

metal washers

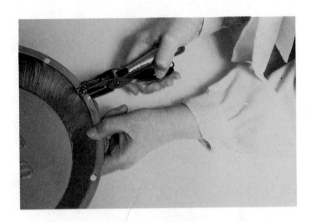

Step 2

She punched holes around the edge of the pan.

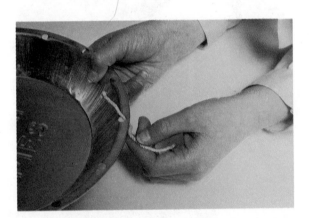

Step 3

She put the string through the holes.

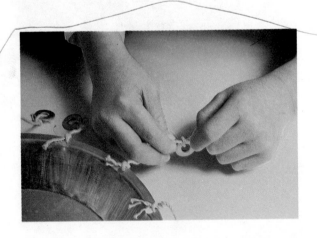

Step 4

She tied the washers to the string.

71

Becky played her tambourine.
It worked! She worked alone
to get what she wanted.

Becky liked playing her
tambourine. But she didn't
like playing alone all the time.
"I want to play in a band,"
Becky said. "But I need others
to do that."

Becky got Bill, Linda, and Fred to join the band. Bill made some cymbals. Linda brought a toy horn. Fred made a drum.

You may get what you need and want alone. Or you may have to work with others.

But you can't always have the things you need or want. You may have too little money to buy them. Or there may not be enough of some things for everyone.

At times like these, you may have to do without. You may have to wait a while. Or you may have to make your own things.

$30.

Brian wanted a big playhouse. But a playhouse cost too much money. He had to get what he wanted in a different way. How did Brian solve his problem?

What Do You Know?

Words to Know
Find the pictures that go with the words.

needs

wants

alone

together

Ideas to Know
Here are pictures of some ways people get things they need and want. Tell about each way you see here.

Using What You Know

Here are pictures of some needs and wants. On a separate piece of paper, make two lists. Call one list "Needs." Call the other list "Wants." Decide whether each thing below is a need or a want. Then write its name on the proper list. Can you think of other needs and wants? Add them to your lists.

Unit 4 Belonging to Groups

79

Lesson 1 Racing Turtles

It was a rainy morning. At first, Patty, Eric, and Philip didn't know what to do. Then Patty had an idea. "Let's make turtles and race them.

"First we'll draw the turtles on heavy
paper. Then, Philip, you cut them out.
Eric, you get some string. We'll cut the
string in pieces four feet long. Then we'll
make a hole in back of the turtle's head.

"Put the string
through the hole.

"Tie the string to
something low.

"Then pull the string
tight. See the turtle
stand?

"Let the string go a
little. The turtle goes
forward."

82

Patty led the group. She helped her
friends have fun on a rainy morning.

At times, you may have led a group just
as Patty did. When do you like to lead
others?

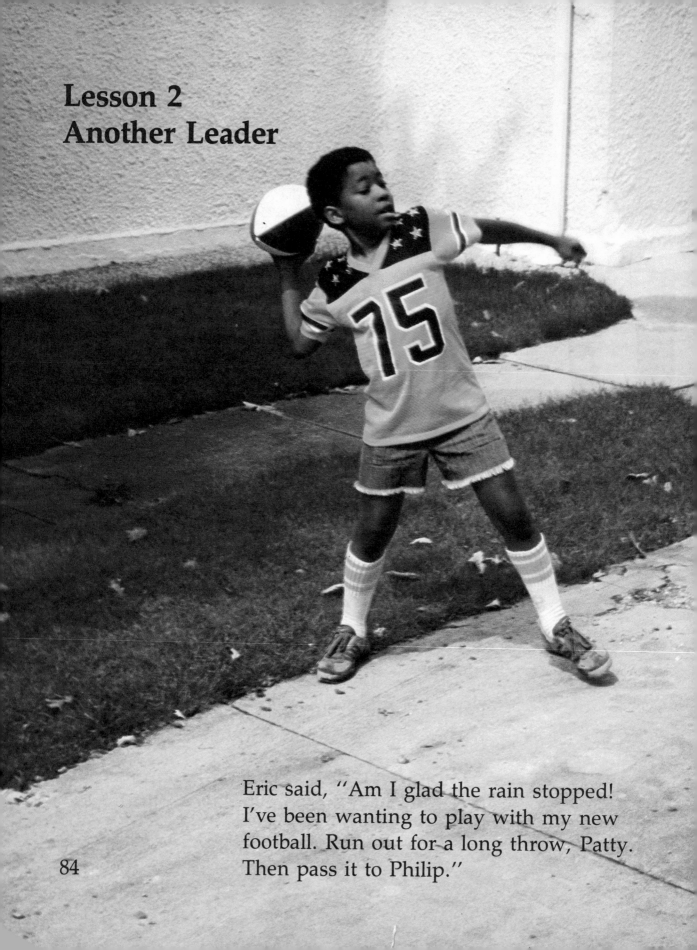

Lesson 2
Another Leader

Eric said, "Am I glad the rain stopped! I've been wanting to play with my new football. Run out for a long throw, Patty. Then pass it to Philip."

Patty led the group in making turtles.
Now Eric is the leader. Philip might want
to lead the group later. That's the way
many groups work. People take turns
leading and following.

Lesson 3   Snowed In

Once Ray went to his grandmother's house during a winter holiday. They planned a happy visit, just the two of them. On the day Ray arrived, snow began to fall.

It snowed for three days. Before Ray and his grandmother knew it, they were snowed in. So was the rest of town. The snow was so heavy it broke the telephone wires. Ray said, "Look, Grandma. The cars and buses can't move."

Grandmother got sick. She had a fever.
Ray tried to call home to his mother and
father. But the wires were down. He
couldn't call a doctor either. So, Ray had
to take care of his grandmother all by
himself.

When Grandmother got well, she said, "Ray, we need some groceries."

"But Grandma, we're snowed in. I can't get to the store."

So, Ray and Grandmother ate leftovers. They drank soft drinks instead of milk.

At last, the snowplow came. Now the telephone repair worker could get to the house. She fixed the wires. Grandmother went to the doctor's office for a checkup. Ray said, "I'll go to the store to get groceries."

Everything turned out all right. On the
last day of the holiday visit, the telephone
rang. It was Ray's mother. She said, "We
heard about the storm. We've tried to call
for days. How are you?"

Ray said, "Grandma got sick. I took care
of her all by myself. We're just fine now."

When You Read

On page 93 is the front page of a newspaper. It tells about a heavy snowstorm that really happened. See what you can learn by reading parts of the newspaper.

Where did the snowstorm happen?
When did it happen?
What do you think the words "Special Blizzard Edition" mean?
Did the storm affect traffic? How?
What accidents happened?
What kinds of places closed because of the storm?

The front page tells about stories in other parts of the paper. See if you can tell where to find the other stories.
What did the President do to help the country fight the storm? On what page can you read the story?

Chicago Daily News

FRIDAY, JANUARY 27, 1978

Metro
Races cancelled
15¢
City and suburb
25¢ Elsewhere

© 1978 BY FIELD ENTERPRISES INC.

A city taken by storm

"However, the storm will come to an end."
—TV weatherman

It was an Anniversary Waltz, a test of character, a proof of nature's power, a pain in the neck. It was a reminder, without ribbons, of the way we were 11 years ago. Just as before, this one beat down from the north and west, came out of the low clouds and whipped the city with its wind and stinging snow and cold, and said it didn't want to stop. The air was gray. The streets drifted over, and were plowed and drifted over again. The highways were reliquaries of abandoned cars. O'Hare closed. The schools closed. The courts closed.

But the weatherman was right, bless him.

The storm came to an end.

Before it melts into memory, while it's still hunched around us and the howling's in our ears, here's the way it was.

Icy tracks blamed for IC crash

Firemen and policemen carry one of 312 victims of Thursday's accident from the Van Buren St. station. RTA officials believe icy tracks caused the crash of two Illinois Central trains. Stories, photos on Pages 3 and 4.

The mood at socked-in O'Hare Airport was: Acapulco can wait. A snowbound city sprang up on the edge of Chicago, full of unexpected friendships. Tall green palm trees stretched toward the ceiling from stone pots in the crimson lobby of the O'Hare Hilton. Cruel winds piled snow higher and higher against the windows. Frankie Ray, piano player in the hotel's Gaslight Club, tinkled out, "Oh, the weather outside is frightful, but the fire is so delightful...."

Two men at the bar munched fish-shaped crackers, sipped Dewar's and soda under a golden-lit oil painting of a nude, and played a game of "Who said that?"

"Who said, 'Unusual weather knits people together'?"

"I give up."

"Mrs. Miniver."

A United Airlines counter girl with the striking name of Heather Wind told a couple, "Your best way to San Juan will be through New York in the morn-
Turn to Page 6

Turn to Page 6

Pedestrian aided after being hit by auto at Randolph and Dearborn. (Daily News Photo/John Tweedle)

Carter sends Army units to Ohio as Midwest digs out from storm
Page 6

La Grange man among 4 victims of severe weather in Illinois
Page 6

Mike Royko: Hip-high snow? It shouldn't happen to a dog
Page 3

Today in the News

The trouble with born-again athletes, says John Schulian, is that "they are approaching religion with the sort of mindless zeal they have devoted to bubblegum and Transcendental Meditation. . . . It is enough to make one wish that the Constitution, which decreed that church and state remain separate, contained the same provision for church and sport." Page 41

A job pinch for college grads could cause serious social upheaval in the next 10 years unless the over-all unemployment problem probably will be curbed, a congressional report says. Page 2

House hunting? If you're planning to buy a new home this year, it's time to start shopping. But first, get some valuable tips in today's special winter Home Life section. "On site" leads it off with a list of the best home buys in the Chicago area. Page 21

Hans W. Mattick died of a self-inflicted gunshot wound, police said. Ironically, the 57-year-old criminologist had pressed for years for strong gun-control legislation. Page 4

Al McGuire tells his best one-liners as he stays in shape for his new job as a basketball commentator. He also explains how to spot a good Mexican restaurant. Page 43

Frigid weekend ahead as the area digs out

By Frank Brennan

Chicago-area residents faced the chilling weekend prospect of bitterly cold temperatures Friday as they dug out from the crippling blizzard that virtually paralyzed traffic and business.

The big Blizzard of '78 officially dumped 12.1 inches of snow on the city, while strong winds tossed up drifts of 5 to 8 feet that left many roads and streets impassable Friday morning.

Schools were closed for the second straight day throughout the Chicago area. Many businesses remained closed, giving employes a long weekend. And snow crews faced the long, cold task of whipping streets into shape for the week ahead before the arrival of any new snow.

But while the snow tapered off to only a few flurries, bitter cold plunged temperatures down to zero levels, with wind chills of 30 below zero. Weekend lows were expected to drop to zero to 10 below, with no warming in sight until Monday.

Thousands of people, either stranded by the storm or unable or unwilling
Turn to Back Page, this section

Turn to Back Page, this section

CTA drivers reject second contract offer

By Dave Canfield

CTA drivers and conductors have rejected a second contract offer, despite predictions by the heads of both transit workers locals that it would be approved by a sizable margin.

Members voted 3,793 to 1,638 against the proposal, which would have provided for a 15-cent-an-hour pay increase retroactive to Dec. 1 and an additional 10-cent-an-hour in-

Union, and Earl Barley Sr., president of Local 241 of the same union, had predicted approval of the new proposal.

"I really don't know why they turned it down," Spears said Friday. He said there is a general feeling of distrust between the management and the union members, which may have contributed to the rejection of what both he and Barley had called a good proposal.

Insight / Thomas J. Foley

After Humphrey, liberals seek leader—and followers

The death of Sen. Hubert Humphrey has put the nation's once-powerful liberal movement on the lookout—for a leader.

Dwindling in numbers and divided in ideology, Democrats on the political left also are searching for an issue to galvanize them once again as a national force.

If they fail, the ideology that has shaped massive changes in the United States since Franklin D. Roosevelt's New Deal days could slowly fade and eventually join the Whigs and other defunct movements in the scrap pile of political philosophy.

While the liberals' quandary has been apparent for some time, the demise of the Minnesota senator on Jan. 13 stirred fresh concern in their ranks.

"The death of Humphrey isn't the death of liberalism, but it is certainly a powerful historical signal," said Fred Dutton, a Washington attorney who was a political confidant to both President John F. Kennedy and his brother Robert.

Pollsters report mounting turmoil within the ranks of those who still describe themselves as liberals—roughly one-third of the American electorate, according to some calculations.

"The next generation after Humphrey must redefine what the liberal positions and agenda should be," said Peter Hart, a professional pollster who tracks voters nationally for liberal candidates and causes. "They will be quite different from that of the 1965-75 period. It's clear we're in a period of transition and haven't found our moorings."

Lacking now is a clear emotional issue, not to mention a liberal champion. In years past, Humphrey's zealous promotion of civil rights epitomized his leadership. For Eugene McCarthy, Robert Kennedy and George McGovern, there was the battle against U.S. involvement in Vietnam.

Mentioned most often as inheriting the leadership are Vice President Walter Mondale, California Gov. Jerry Brown, Rep. Morris Udall (D-Ariz.) and Senators Edward M. Kennedy (D-Mass.), Gary Hart (D-Colo.) and Dick Clark (D-Iowa).

Lesson 4   Eduardo's Community

94

Eduardo and his sister, Isabel, live in Casares, Spain. It's a small town where most people know each other. Eduardo and Isabel have many friends there.

Casares is on a mountain. Eduardo must
climb a steep hill to get to his house.

Today it was Eduardo's job to carry the
wash up the hill. It was too heavy for him
alone. Isabel had to help. They often help
with work around the house.

Eduardo's mother is preparing
dinner. Tonight she's cooking
seafood stew, Eduardo's favorite
meal. She often tries to fix
her family's favorites. They
depend on her for many things.

Eduardo and some of his
friends belong to the town's
marching band. Eduardo
missed practice one day.
His friends said the music
didn't sound the same
without him.

On Sunday after church, the people of
Casares often meet in the village square.
They go there to talk and find out the
latest news.

Like Eduardo, you belong to many groups. One is your family group. Another is your community. In both groups, people depend on each other in many ways.

101

What Do You Know?

Words to Know

Find the pictures that go with the words.

family

depend

lead

follow

Ideas to Know

Here are pictures of people in your community. Tell how people depend on them. Tell how they depend on others.

Using What You Know

Below is a story about how a boy depended on his mother and father. Use the clues to read the story.

Willie went ice -ing with his father.

The 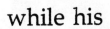 was thin and broke. Willie

fell through. His father threw Willie a .

Willie hung on to the  while his

father pulled him out of the cold 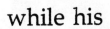.

At home, Willie sat by the . His

mother gave him warm, dry

to wear. She fixed him a of hot milk.

Unit 5 Alike and Different

Lesson 1
Games Around the World

In Holland, children play a follow-the-leader game called Windmill.

106

In China, they like
to play a game called
Kick the Rope.

107

Children in Mexico like to jump rope.

In Indonesia, children sometimes play baseball.

Children from different parts of the world may not look just the same. They may dress differently and play different games. But one thing is the same. Almost all children like to get together in groups and play games that are fun.

Can you think of other things that are the same?

Lesson 2   Family Groups

A Riddle

Some are big, and
      some are small.
Some are young, and
      some are old.
Some have dads,
      some have moms, and
      some have both.
Some have children
      in them, and
      some have none.
Into some, children
      are born; in others
      they are chosen.
What are they?

How are these families alike?

How are they different?

How are Albert's and Juanita's families alike? How are they different?

Lesson 3 Something New

Sometimes families are alike. Sometimes families are different. They may have different numbers of people in them. They may do things in different ways.

People can be alike or different, too. Look at Bob. Like many children, Bob likes to play with toys. Today he got two new toy trucks.

116

But Bob is different. Not many children his age have typewriters. This is a special typewriter. Bob needs it to do his school work.

Bob cannot see. Sometimes he plays and works differently from others. But he knows that almost everyone is different from others in one way or another.

When You Read

Pretend you are a detective. Here are some clues. Use the clues to finish the sentences.

Susan has a bag of marbles. Tommy has some chalk. He is drawing a large circle on the walk. They are going to

_____ .

Sarah had her dog, Angus, in her arms. Father had the warm water ready. Soap and towels were nearby. Father and Sarah were going to

_____ .

The stars were out. The moon was shining brightly. Most people were in bed. It was _____ .

Juan put on his heavy coat and cap. Next he put on his warm boots and mittens. He was ready to go outdoors. It was a _____ .

The monkey families were swinging on their ropes. Anna heard a lion roar in its cage. Anna was at

_____ .

119

Lesson 4   The Long Recess

Debbie has a lot of friends. They always do things together. At school they always play together during recess.

Just as the recess bell rang one day, Julie had an idea. "Let's not go in. Let's stay out here and play."

120

"OK!" and they all began to scatter.

Debbie just stood there looking worried. "Hey, Debbie," yelled Julie. "Are you with us or not?"

Debbie didn't know what to do.

What might Debbie do?

121

What Do You Know?

Words to Know

Find the pictures that go with the words.

alike

different

playgroup

Ideas to Know

Look at these pictures of groups and decide what kinds of groups they are. How are these groups like your own? How are they different?

What groups do you belong to?

Using What You Know

Here are some people with problems. They need help from other people. Tell how their groups can help them.

—Alfredo got a low grade in spelling.

—Carlos is a new boy in school and doesn't know his way around.

—Alice has just been chosen leader of her group.

—Maria has broken her arm in a fall.

—Renee just got scolded and feels bad.

123

Unit **6** Being Yourself in Groups

125

Lesson 1 · Ricardo

126

¡Hola! Me llamo Ricardo.
Hello! My name is Ricardo.
I was born in the United
States, but my parents are
from Mexico. I speak
English like most of my
friends, but I also speak
Spanish.

Sometimes at school, I'd
forget an English word.
So I said it in Spanish.
My friends laughed at me.

One day at school we
studied about the state of
Florida. I told my friends
that in Spanish, *Florida*
means "full of flowers."
They all want to go there
now.

One time, we had burritos for lunch at school. "Ugh! What's that?" Herbie asked. I told him it was a thin pancake with meat and refried beans inside. "Try it," I said, "it tastes good." Herbie got a burrito and loved it.

Another time, a famous baseball player came
to visit our class. He asked if anyone could
speak Spanish. "I can, I can," I said. You
should have seen my friends look at me then. 129

FIGHT DISEASE
KEEP
CLEAN
S EEP
RCISE
AT THE
RIGHT
FOODS

WHERE THERE'S SMOKE...
THERE SHOULD BE
A SMOKE ALARM

130

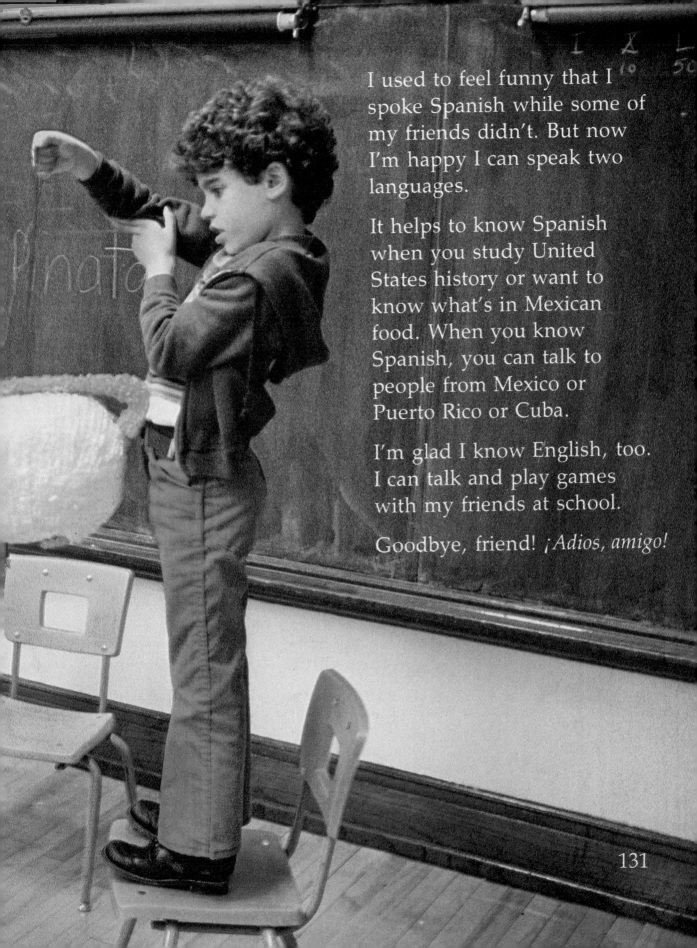

I used to feel funny that I spoke Spanish while some of my friends didn't. But now I'm happy I can speak two languages.

It helps to know Spanish when you study United States history or want to know what's in Mexican food. When you know Spanish, you can talk to people from Mexico or Puerto Rico or Cuba.

I'm glad I know English, too. I can talk and play games with my friends at school.

Goodbye, friend! *¡Adios, amigo!*

131

Lesson 2
A Community Problem

In her family, Laura has the job of taking out the trash. Sometimes she doesn't throw the trash into the cans carefully.

The trash collectors remove the trash from the cans. Sometimes they aren't careful. They spill trash on the ground, too.

Other people in the community have this problem, too. The community is beginning to look messy. The people talk about their problem at a community meeting. They see that what they do with trash is important. They want a clean community.

What rules might help the people solve their problem?

133

Community Workers

A community needs a lot of workers to get things done. Look at the pictures. See if you can name the jobs the community workers are doing.

135

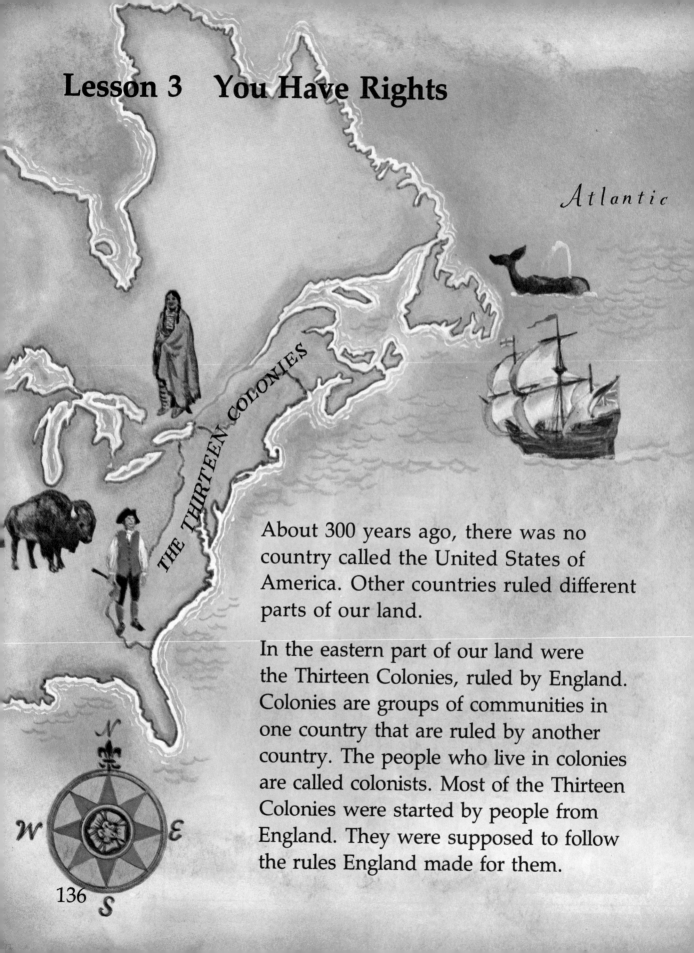

Lesson 3   You Have Rights

Atlantic

THE THIRTEEN COLONIES

About 300 years ago, there was no country called the United States of America. Other countries ruled different parts of our land.

In the eastern part of our land were the Thirteen Colonies, ruled by England. Colonies are groups of communities in one country that are ruled by another country. The people who live in colonies are called colonists. Most of the Thirteen Colonies were started by people from England. They were supposed to follow the rules England made for them.

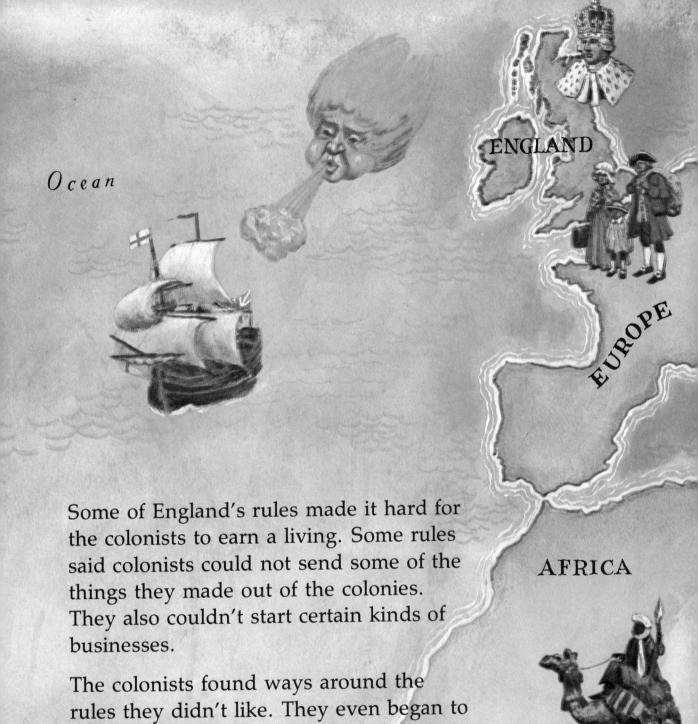

Ocean

ENGLAND

EUROPE

AFRICA

Some of England's rules made it hard for the colonists to earn a living. Some rules said colonists could not send some of the things they made out of the colonies. They also couldn't start certain kinds of businesses.

The colonists found ways around the rules they didn't like. They even began to make some of their own rules. England was far away. It had other problems to worry about. So it didn't always force the colonists to follow its rules.

137

Then England needed money. So it decided to tax the colonists without asking them. This meant that when the people bought things like sugar or cloth, they had to pay more for them. This extra money went to England.

Many colonists thought this was not fair. They thought they should help make any rules they had to follow. They believed they had the right to decide these things for themselves.

England and the colonists could not agree. Finally they went to war against each other.

The colonists needed someone to lead their armies against England. They asked George Washington. Washington believed strongly in the colonists' right to decide things for themselves.

But it was a hard choice for Washington. He hated to leave his farm in Virginia. Besides that, many people thought the colonists couldn't win. They didn't have much money to pay for a war. England had a big army. The colonists did not. They didn't even have many guns or warm clothes or food.

139

140

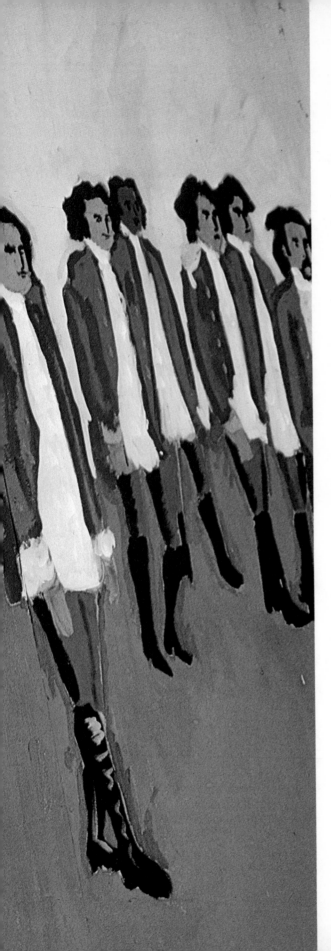

Finally Washington said yes.
He led the army for five years.
After a long, hard fight, the
colonists finally won. They
were no longer ruled by
England. They had won the
right to rule themselves.

They chose their brave leader,
George Washington, to be the
first President of their new
country, the United States of
America.

The American people had
fought for the right to rule
themselves. Some had even
died for that right.

There are many kinds of rights.
You have a right to be happy.
You have a right to have fun
during recess.

Today Americans believe that
all people have a right to be
free. One hundred years ago,
some people didn't have that
right. Harriet Tubman was one
of those people.

The Right to Be Free

Harriet Tubman was born a slave in Maryland about 1821. Slaves are people who are not free. They are forced to work for other people. They must do what others order. On most days, Harriet heard words like these. "Harriet, carry water to the workers in the fields!" "Harriet, clean the house!" "Harriet, watch the baby!"

A law said that Harriet Tubman's people, black Americans who were slaves, could not learn to read and write. But she learned other things. She called one of her teachers Daddy Ben. Daddy Ben taught her about the forest and the stars. "These berries are safe to eat, but not those." "That is the North Star. You always know where north is when you see that star."

143

Harriet Tubman grew into a woman who hated being a slave. She thought, "People should have the right to be free. No one should be a slave."

So, one night, Harriet Tubman ran away.

As she ran, Harriet Tubman used what Daddy Ben taught her. She ate berries so she wouldn't starve. The North Star led her to Pennsylvania, a state where people couldn't have slaves. Later Harriet Tubman returned to Maryland many times. She showed other slaves the way to freedom.

145

Americans disagreed about owning slaves. Some Americans thought it was right for people to have slaves. Other Americans agreed with Harriet Tubman. They said, "No person should have to be a slave." Americans went to war again. Finally, slavery was ended.

When You Read

Suppose you were going to write about the things George Washington did. Some of the sentences below tell some of the things he did for his country. Some of them do not.

Which sentences tell what George Washington did for his country?

—George Washington became the first President of the United States of America.

—He was born on February 22, 1732.

—He had a farm in Virginia.

—He led an army to help the colonists win their rights.

—He had dark brown hair when he was young.

—He believed strongly in the colonists' right to decide things for themselves.

—He was over six feet tall.

What Do You Know?

Words to Know

Find the pictures that go with the words.

community

colonist

tax

148

Ideas to Know

Use the drawings to help you name some jobs people do in your community.

Using What You Know

What rights do these people have?

Ellen has a diary that she wants kept secret. She caught her little brother reading it. Tell about Ellen's rights.

David is playing a game with some friends. When it's his turn to play, someone says, "David doesn't get a turn. Let's skip him and go on to the next person." Tell about David's rights.

Santino had been standing in the lunch line a long time. Just as he gets to the head of the line, someone cuts in front of him. Tell about Santino's rights.

149

Unit 7 Making Changes

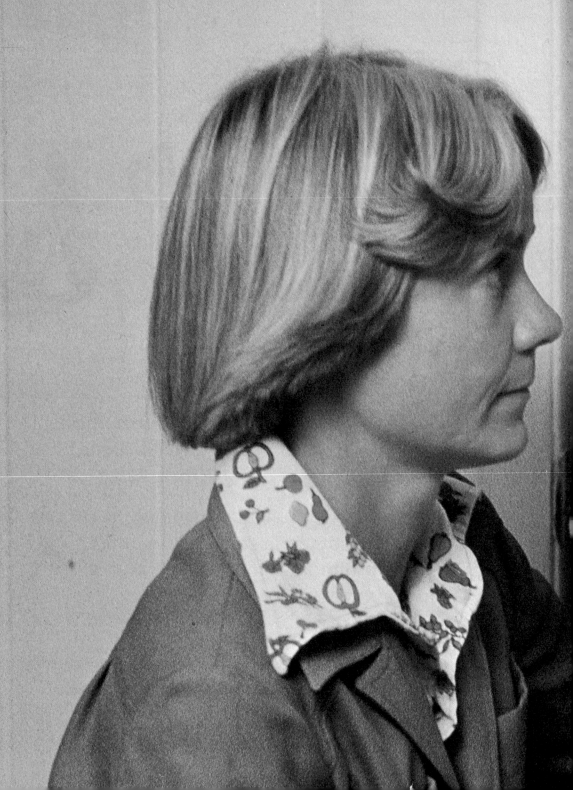

150

151

Lesson 1 The Way Things Used to Be: A Play

Ruthie: I wish everything was the way it used to be.

Mother: What do you mean, Ruthie?

Ruthie: Ever since you went back to work, the family hasn't been the same.

Father: Your mother is working because we need the money, Ruth.

Mother: Not only that, I like my work.

Ruthie: But we rush so much in the mornings now. We never get to eat breakfast all together.

Jimmy: Ruthie's right. Mom is too tired to play games with us at night like before. We never go for walks anymore.

Ruthie: Daddy never makes dessert for
   our dinner. Why can't things be the
   way they were?
Mother: You and Jimmy are old enough
   to do lots of things on your own. I
   feel I can work away from home
   now.

Ruthie: I know the family has changed.
But it'd be good to keep some things
the same as before.

Father: What things?

Ruthie: How about if we all get up a little
earlier in the mornings and eat
breakfast together!

Jimmy: If I help do dishes
after dinner every night,
could we play some games
and take walks together?

Mother: I think we can do
that.

Father: Maybe some night
instead of playing games,
we can make those
desserts you miss.

Ruthie: If we can keep some
of the good things the
way they were, then the
changes won't be so bad.

Over the years, all people
change in some ways. So do
their groups. Sometimes
changes are for the best,
sometimes not. Often people
choose to make the best of
the changes in their lives.
They let changes come. But
they try not to lose the good
parts of the way things were.

Lesson 2 Mike's Report

Mike used to throw empty glass bottles away. One day Greg stopped him. He said, "Don't you know you can get money for those?"

Greg told Mike about a program he saw on television. The program told how workers at a glass factory melted old bottles and used them again to make new ones. "They call that 'recycling,'" Greg said.

159

The glass company paid one cent for every three used bottles turned in. Mike thought, "I'm going to find out more about this." At school, Mike studied about recycling and reported what he had learned to the class.

RECYCLING

Mike said, "Recycling is good for four reasons:

1. Recycling saves natural resources.
2. Recycling keeps people from putting used bottles in unsafe places.
3. Recycling can help people earn money.
4. Recycling keeps towns and cities looking clean."

Learning about recycling changed Mike's feeling about throwing empty bottles away.

A Class Project

After Mike made his report, Mary said, "Let's collect used glass bottles. We could clean up our neighborhood and earn money, too."

Mike said, "What should we do with the money we earn?"

Miss Denker said, "I read in the newspaper that the town needs more trees. You could use the money you earn to buy seedlings and plant them. Imagine how each of you could help change the town. You could make it clean and beautiful."

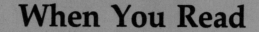

When You Read

Let's study some information about the project started by Mike's class. Read the information as you would any sentence, from left to right.

Second Grade Clean-up Project
First Week

COLUMN 1	COLUMN 2	COLUMN 3
Names	**Bottles**	**Cents**
Carol	9	.03
Lisa	18	.06
Jay	3	.01
Julio	12	.04
Ted	6	.02
Mary	24	.08
Kathy	15	.05
Jill	100	.33
Mike	30	.10
Greg	21	.07
Totals	**238**	**.79**

Column 1 tells the names of the children who joined the project. Column 2 tells how many bottles each child brought in a week. Column 3 tells how much money each child earned. Under the double line are the total number of bottles and the total amount of money earned.

Answer these questions:

1. Who brought in the most bottles?
2. Who brought in the fewest bottles?
3. What four children seem to be most interested in the project? How can you tell?
4. Suppose the children continued their project for ten weeks and brought in the same number of bottles each week. How many bottles would they have brought in at the end of the project? How much money would they have earned?

Lesson 3   The Wild Horses

Have you ever pretended to be a horse? If you have, were you faster than any other animal? Did you pretend to run across open spaces, no fences to stop you? Mustangs are horses like that.

Mustangs live in the open, unsettled lands of the western United States. Once the mustangs numbered in the millions. But then people learned that they could make money by catching the mustangs.

They put the mustangs in trucks and took them to factories. There, workers killed the animals and made them into pet food. By the 1970s, there were only a few thousand mustangs left alive. If those died, there would be no wild horses left in the United States.

The children of Miss Bolsinger's class, a class just like yours, heard about the danger to the mustangs. "People shouldn't treat wild animals like that!" they said. The children wrote letters to other school children. They wrote, "Help us save the mustangs!"

Other children agreed with those in Miss Bolsinger's class. Lots of other Americans did, too. They formed a big group that wanted to save the mustangs. The group wrote to lawmakers in Washington, D.C., asking for help. Two children even went to talk with the lawmakers.

170

The lawmakers listened. Then they argued with each other for a long time. Some said, "We should protect the mustangs." Others said, "The mustangs aren't important enough for us to worry about." Finally, most lawmakers agreed to make rules, or laws, protecting mustangs on public land.

171

HOW IS A LAW MADE IN WASHINGTON?

Groups of people tell lawmakers what they want.

If some of the lawmakers think the groups have a good idea, they write up a bill.

172

In small groups,
the lawmakers talk
about the bill.

They listen to people tell what they
think about the bill.

The lawmakers vote.
If most lawmakers vote yes,
the bill becomes an act.

The lawmakers send the act to the President. If the President thinks the act would be a good law, he signs it. Then the act becomes a law.

That is how a group of Americans made a law to save the mustangs.

Why do you think lawmakers listen, talk, and argue when they make laws like the one to save the mustangs?

175

What Do You Know?

Words to Know
Find the pictures that go with the words.

change

recycling

law

lawmakers

Ideas to Know
On the next page are pictures of many things. They show how people change. Tell at what time during someone's life he or she would probably use these things. Use the words "As a child," "As a teen-ager," and "As a grown-up" for your answers.

Things to wear:

Things to read:

Things to ride:

Things to put together:

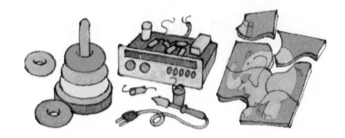

Using What You Know

Here are two pictures of a community. One shows the community many years ago. One shows it today. Describe how the community changed between then and now.

Handbook of Skills and Information

Getting New Information   179

Practicing Map and Globe Skills   182-193

Words to Know   194-197

Index   198-199

Acknowledgments   200

Getting New Information

Do you remember reading the story about Mr. Lucky Straw? That story was about a boy named Shobei. He lived in the country of Japan.

Find the continent of Asia in this picture of a globe. Now find Japan. It is a country of many islands. An island is land that has water all around it. Four of these islands are quite large. Others are very small.

Japan lies off the east coast of Asia. To the west is the Sea of Japan. To the east lies the Pacific Ocean.

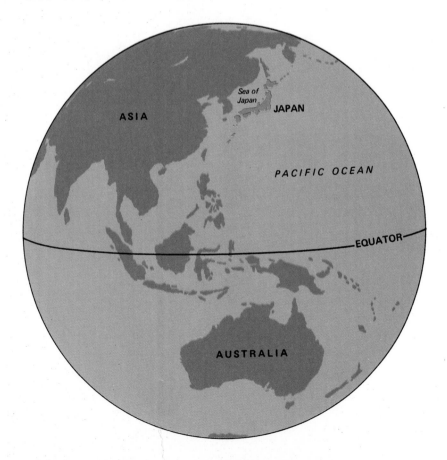

Do you remember reading about Eduardo and his sister Isabel? They live in the country of Spain.

Find the continent of Europe in this picture of a globe. Now find Spain. Spain is in the southwestern part of Europe.

Spain has two neighbors in Europe. France is to the north of Spain. Where is Portugal? Spain is also near Africa.

Spain is almost surrounded by water. It lies between the Atlantic Ocean and the Mediterranean Sea. Eduardo and Isabel live in the village of Casares. It is very close to the Mediterranean Sea.

Do you remember reading about Ricardo? He was born in the United States, but his parents came from Mexico.

Find the continent of North America in this picture of a globe. Now find Mexico. Mexico is a country in the southern part of North America. It lies just south of the United States. Mexico is also near South America.

Mexico lies between two oceans. To the east is the Gulf of Mexico. It is part of the Atlantic Ocean. To the west of Mexico is the Pacific Ocean.

Practicing Map and Globe Skills

All people live on Earth. You live on Earth. All your friends live on Earth.

A globe is a model of Earth. The shape of Earth is round. A globe is round. A globe shows the shape of Earth.

There is land and water on Earth. You live on land. How can you tell the land from the water in this picture of a globe?

The black line going around the globe is the Equator. What does the Equator do?

Large bodies of land are called continents. Continents are different sizes. Some continents are larger than others. Continents have different shapes.

A globe shows where the continents are on Earth. A globe shows the size and shape of the continents. What are the names of the continents?

North America is a continent. You live in North America. Is North America the same size as the other continents? Is North America the same shape as the other continents?

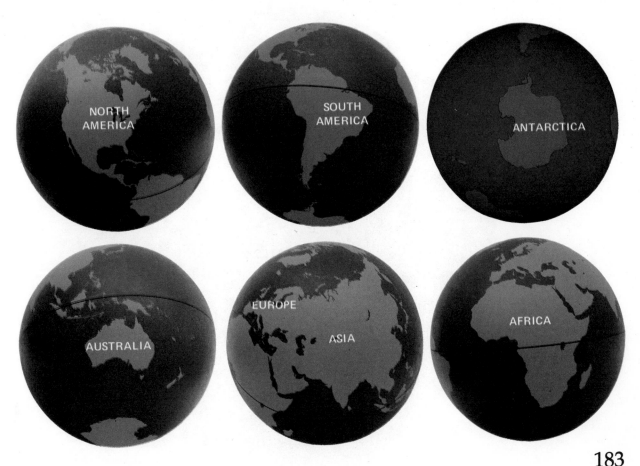

Your local community is in the United States of America. The United States of America is very large, but it is not as large as North America.

Look at this picture of a globe. It shows all of North America. The three parts of the United States are yellow. Canada and Mexico are light green. How do you know that the United States is not the same size as the continent of North America?

Can you find the place where you live on the globe?

This is a map. It shows most of the United States of America. What is missing from the United States? Does the map have the same shape as a globe?

The United States is yellow. The black lines that cross it show where the states begin and end. Can you find the place where you live on the map?

Canada and Mexico are also in North America. They are light green. Canada is north of the United States. Is Mexico north or south of the United States? How can you tell?

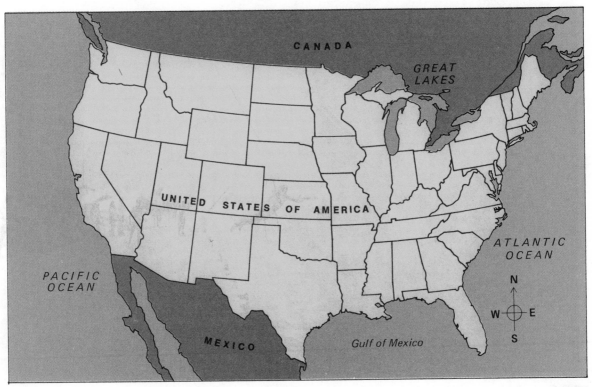

The largest bodies of water on Earth are called oceans. Oceans have names just as continents have names.

Look at the map on page 185. What is the name of the ocean to the east of the United States? What is the name of the ocean to the west of the United States? How can you tell?

A lake is a body of water with land all around it. A lake is much smaller than an ocean. Can you find any lakes on the map?

A river is a body of water, too. The water in a river flows from a higher to a lower place. A river begins where the land is high and flows to a body of water that is lower.

This is a map of the eastern part of the United States. Find the rivers on the map. Find the place where the Mississippi River flows into a large body of water. Can you find the place where the Mississippi River begins? Does the river flow north or south?

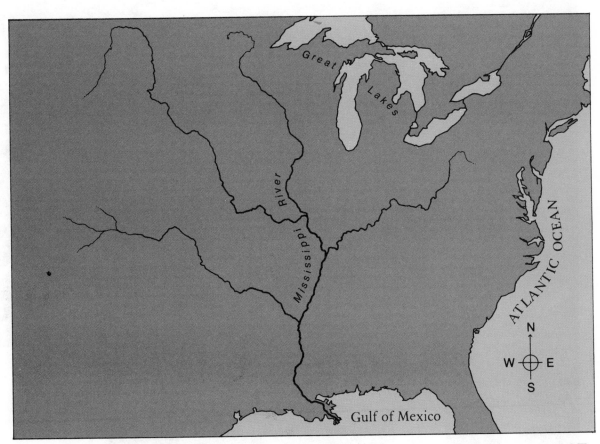

This is a picture of a town. What can you learn from the picture?

This is a map of the same town. Do the map and the picture look alike?

On the map, symbols are used to show some things. A symbol is a sign that stands for something. A symbol may be used to stand for a building, a street, or a river. Can you find some symbols on the map? What do they stand for? Where is north on the map? How can you tell?

Key

🜄 Water tower

✝ Church

👢 Fire Station

▱ Railroad track

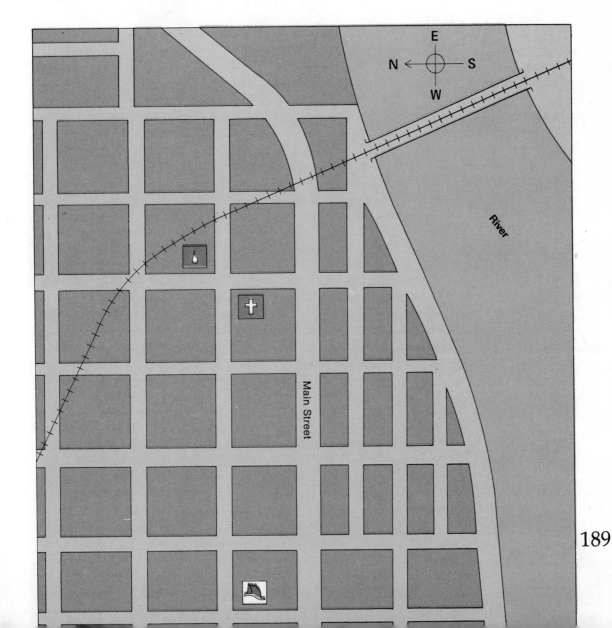

River

Main Street

189

This is a picture of a part of a city. A city is bigger than a town. Many people live and work in a city. What can you see in the picture?

This is a map of the same part of the city. Do the map and the picture look alike or different?

On this map, symbols are also used. The box on the map tells you what some of the symbols mean. This box is a map key. What does each symbol mean? Find each symbol on the map. Where is north on the map? How can you tell?

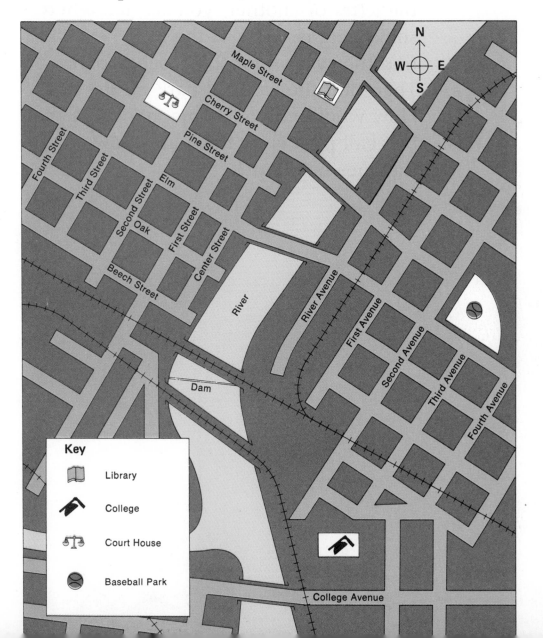

Maple Street

Cherry Street

Pine Street

Elm

Oak

Fourth Street

Third Street

Second Street

First Street

Center Street

Beech Street

River

Dam

River Avenue

First Avenue

Second Avenue

Third Avenue

Fourth Avenue

N
W E
S

Key

Library

College

Court House

Baseball Park

College Avenue

On the opposite page is another map of the same city. How are the two maps alike? How are the two maps different?

Lines have been added to this map of the city. Some of the lines go from west to east. These lines have numbers. Some of the lines go from north to south. These lines have letters.

If you know the number of one line and the letter of another, you can tell where something is. Look at the map key and find the symbol for the baseball park. Then find the baseball park on the map. How would you tell someone where the baseball park is on the map? How would the lines help you?

MAP OF CITY

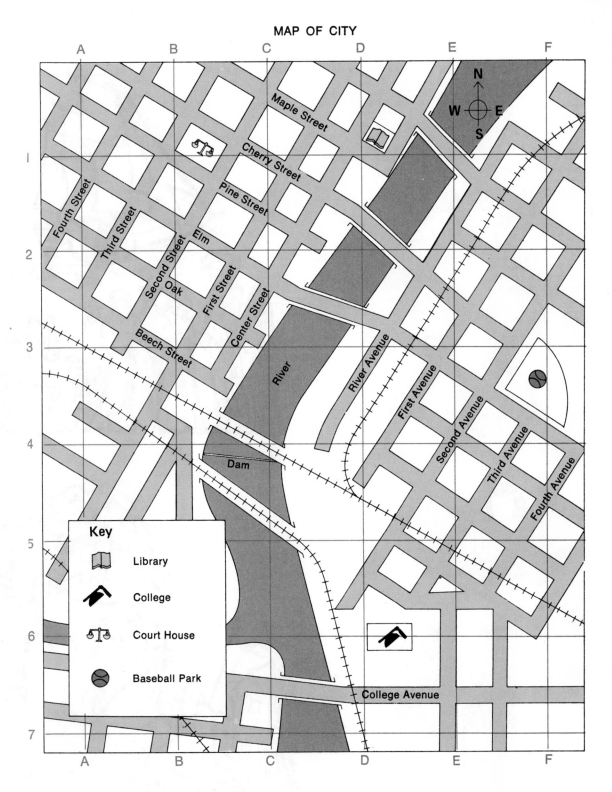

Key
- Library
- College
- Court House
- Baseball Park

193

Words to Know

alike

colonist

alone

community

change

194

depend

family

different

follow

directions

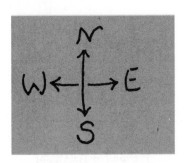

friends

happy

lead

law

lonely

lawmakers

map

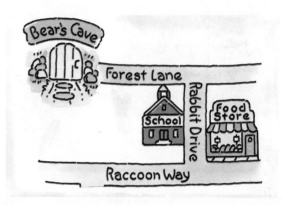

needs

recycling

neighbor

tax

playgroup

together

wants

proud

197

Index

A

Americans, and rights, 136–137, 139, 141. *See also* Black Americans; Civil War; Tubman, Harriet; Washington, George.

B

Black Americans, 142. *See also* Civil War; Tubman, Harriet.

C

careers, doctor, 90; telephone repair worker, 90; *illus.* 134–135, firefighter, letter carrier, librarian, police officer, school bus driver, teacher, veterinarian
Casares, Spain, 98, 100; family, 96–97; *illus.* 95–101
change, in family groups, 153–157
China, play in, 107; *illus.* 107
Civil War, 146
colonies, thirteen English, 136–140
community, 132–133; in Casares, Spain, 98, 100; *illus.* 94–95. *See also* careers.

D

differences, in people, 114–117
directions, 38–43

F

family, and influence, 12–13, 44–47, 50–51; dependence on, 67, 97, 101; and work, 68, 96–97; *illus.* 96, 97, 100–101; differences among, 110–113
feelings, 16–19
Florida, Spanish word, 127
following, in groups, 80–85
friends, in Casares, Spain, 98; dependence on, 67; and influence, 48, 120–121; *illus.* 48, 67, 98–99, 120–121

G

games, in other countries, 106–109. *See also* China, Holland, Indonesia, Mexico.
groups, in Casares, Spain, 98, 100; community, 98, 100, 101; family, 110–114; friends, 83, 85; *illus.* 98–99, 100–101, 110–114

H

Holland, play in, 106; *illus.* 106
horses. *See* mustangs.

I

Indonesia, play in, 108; *illus.* 109

J

Japanese folktale, 56-60

L

law, how a law is made, 172–175
lawmakers, 170–175
leading, in groups, 80–85

M

Maryland, Harriet Tubman in, 142–144, 145
Mexican American, at school, 124–131; *illus.* 124–131
Mexico, play in, 108; Spanish spoken in, 131; *illus.* 108, 128. *See also* Mexican American.
mustangs, 166, 169; laws to save, 171, 175; children influence laws about, 169–171; *illus.* 167–168

N

needs and wants, 61, 64, 67, 72–75, 89; *def.* 61
neighbors, influence of, 49
newspaper, how to read articles in, 92–93

P

Pennsylvania, law against slave ownership in, 145; Harriet Tubman's escape to, 145
play, 5, 7, 8, 9, 11, 120–121; differences in, 114–117; *illus.* 2–5, 7–8, 10–11, 114–117, 120–121. *See also* China, Holland, Indonesia, Mexico.
Puerto Rico, Spanish spoken in, 131

R

recycle, 158–161
rights, 139, 141, 144, 146

Spain, Casares, 95–96, 100; *illus.* 94–101
Spanish, language of Cuba, Mexico, Puerto Rico, 131; phrases, 127, 131. *See also* Florida, Mexican American.

T

Thirteen Colonies, as English colonies, 136–139; at war with England, 139–141; gain their independence, 141; *map,* 136–137
time, understanding, 26–27
Tubman, Harriet, 142–146; *illus.* 142–146

W

wants. *See* needs and wants.
Washington, George, 139, 141, 147; *illus.* 140
wildlife, 30–31
work, 6, 9, 68; differences in, 116–117; in family, 68, 96–97; of young Harriet Tubman, 142; *illus.* 6, 9, 96, 97, 116–117, 142

Z

zoo, 26–29; *illus.* 24–29

Acknowledgments

Illustrations
Cover Seasons in the City Mural, 51st and Lake Park, Painted by Hyde Park Children, Chicago, Ill. **30–31** Stouffer Productions Ltd., ANIMALS ANIMALS. **34–35** Harald Sund. **35 (bottom)** Josef Muench. **36–37** Larry Keenan Jr., NEST. **37 (top)** Jacques Jangoux from Peter Arnold. **37 (center)** Erik Arnesen. **37 (bottom)** Grant Heilman. **93** Courtesy of The Chicago Daily News. **107** John Dominis, Life Magazine, © Time Inc. **108** Erik Arnesen. **109** Harrison Forman. **134** Richard Capps, R/C Photo Agency. **166–167** Hope Ryden, ANIMALS ANIMALS. **168–169** Courtesy of WHOA! (Wild Horse Organized Assistance).

Quoted Material
16 "Lonely." From ALL ON A SUMMER'S DAY, by William Wise. Copyright © 1971 by William Wise. Reprinted by permission of Pantheon Books, a Division of Random House, Inc. and Curtis Brown, Ltd. **27** "Time Passes" from I WATCH THE WORLD GO BY by Ilo Orleans. Copyright © 1961 by Ilo Orleans. Reprinted by permission of Friede Orleans Joffe. **50–51** Words and Music of "Little Arabella Miller" from EYE WINKER, TOM TINKER, CHIN CHOPPER, FIFTY MUSICAL FINGERPLAYS by Tom Glazer, published by Doubleday & Company, Inc. Copyright © 1973, Songs Music, Inc., Scarborough, N.Y. 10510. Reprinted by permission of Tom Glazer. **56–63** From "Mr. Lucky Straw" from JAPANESE CHILDREN'S FAVORITE STORIES, edited by Florence Sakade. Copyright © 1958 by Charles E. Tuttle Company, Inc. Reprinted by permission. **80–83** Adaptation of "Cardboard Racing Turtles." From MAKING THINGS: The Hand Book of Creative Discovery by Ann Wiseman. Copyright © 1973 by Ann Wiseman. Reprinted by permission of Little, Brown and Co.